Made in United States
Orlando, FL
28 April 2022

17180458R00067